D1478583

The Bad Guys

Paul Hostovsky

FUTURECYCLE PRESS
www.futurecycle.org

Library of Congress Control Number: 2015939549

Published by FutureCycle Press
Lexington, Kentucky, USA

ISBN 978-1-938853-77-7

To *all* the bad guys, with love

Contents

I.

II.

Acknowledgments

I.

In the Home for Elderly Vehicular Manslaughterers by the Sea

The guilt, like the sand, is in everything,
being so near, as they are, to the ocean,
being so close, as they were, to the end
of their lives, before they took the lives
they took. Someone should have taken
the keys away. In many cases, they tried—
but the old, mottled, gnarled knuckles
clenched, closing reflexively around
that silver promise, its heft, its glinting
mountainous teeth. And they held on to it.
Now the guilt, like the sand, is on their hands
and on their lips. It's the grit in the food
they can't eat. Lucky the demented ones,
with no idea, no memory, blithely chewing.

To the Lady Who Gave Out Pencils on Halloween

I would like to say thank you,
because I don't think I said thank you
once in all those years
that I climbed your steep front steps
in my mask or sheet or wig or witch's hat
and held up my opened pillow case
among the other opened pillow cases
like so many straining baby-bird mouths
in the hope that you would finally come around
to our sweet-tooth point of view. Which you never did.
So we mocked you, and we spurned you,
and we littered your lawn with our candy wrappers,
our chewed gum the sweet had gone out of,
the rinds and sticks of the much-lauded,
much-coveted candied apples your neighbor
Mrs. Schachtel gave out each year—the syrupy
antithesis to your dry and austere
number two pencils. But they survived,
it needs to be said—when all that sugary
frivolity melted away, your stiffly formal
wooden gifts remained, like so many horizontal
soldiers standing at attention at the bottom
of the bag. Deployed in kitchen drawers,
desk drawers, jars jammed with pens, pencils,
brushes, penknives, magic markers, emery boards,
they were mostly overlooked, forgotten. Some of them
probably outlived my entire childhood. A few
probably outlived you. It's entirely possible
that one or two—this one, for example,
which feels as sharp as the day it was first
sharpened—could outlive me, too.

To the Man Talking to Himself
on a Park Bench

Could it be, Delirius, that it's left to you
to say out loud what the rest of us
are all just thinking to ourselves,
in so many words? If not the gist of it
then the thrust of it, the spill of it, the raging
waterfall of it? You are vaguely dangerous
with your amblyopic eye, your mossy beard
caked with dirt and crumbs and life-forms that crawl
and fly. But what frightens me isn't you.
It's the danger of going where you have gone,
of opening that door, that window,
and not being able to close it now,
all the interior monologue flying out,
flying free. I envy you that freedom in a way,
the going over that waterfall
with nothing but the broken staves of your own
rotten teeth framing your verbal free fall,
the relinquishment of resistance, the syllables
of all your enthusiasms, imprecations,
recitations and improvisations like so much
spray misting above that vertiginous
ecstatic abandon. And the faint illusion
of a rainbow hanging in the air just above your head.
No, what frightens me isn't you, Delirius.
It's that slatted green bench right next to yours,
looking so vacant, so unoccupied, and so free.

Slapstick

The three stooges weren't funny anymore
after Kenny Hovanek stopped me in the park
and slapped me in the face and knocked
my books down. Suddenly Moe looked
a lot like Hitler without the mustache.
And Larry and Curly looked like
what I must have looked like to Kenny Hovanek
who chuckled sadistically, shook his head, swaggered
away. My cheek stung for days. My father
went on chuckling right there beside me
on the paisley couch in front of our television,
but our favorite show had changed forever
and I couldn't tell him why. If I laughed now
it was a forced laugh, so he wouldn't know
I'd met force in the park, met it with nothing
but tears. Which hurt more than the blow.
It was torture, sitting there next to him,
laughing at the pain, laughing through the pain,
but I never cracked: I never said a word.

Smelly Poem

What is that evil stench, you ask yourself,
looking around for its source, its etiology, its home,
if smells can be said to have homes.
It's a homeless sort of smell, a sodden-
socks, ratty-sneakers, urine-in-a-doorway
sort of smell. You don't suppose
it could be coming from that beautiful woman
with the flawless skin and excellent teeth
laughing and talking with that tawny gentleman
in the sensible shoes, do you? Anything
is possible—anyone could have
a leaky urostomy bag or suppurating leg infection
going on underneath. You yourself
could have bad-tooth breath and not even know it.
That evil stench could be yours; it could be you.
You could have stepped in a small death, the kind
your dog loves to roll around in, and brought it
home with you, wrapped in it now like a shawl.

In Praise of Poor Excuses

Blessed are the poor excuses
for they are inherently of earth—
earth, that poor excuse for heaven—
heaven, that worst excuse of all
for not showing up for your own
life here on earth, where all the poor excuses
live. Just listen to the poor excuses
singing together, hoisting another
draft of a poor excuse up to their lips
and spilling it down their shirtfronts,
and laughing the loudest, and telling
the biggest whoppers. And what on earth
are we to make of all the poor excuses
that we make here on earth? I say:
praise them. For they are in the world
and of it. For they are falling from the lips
like so many colorful, beautiful, pathetic
dead leaves dancing down and no one
is using them for anything except
maybe the children, and here and there
a few suspicious-looking grown-ups
gathering them into piles, into poems,
and digging around in them till evening comes,
and heading home with one or two
still sticking to their heads.

Hitler Stamp

I traded ten triangular
Mongolian stamps for Hitler,
Hitler who killed my father's
whole family.

My father hated Hitler.
He refused to say Hitler's name.
He refused to let anyone say it
under his roof. He refused

to speak a word of German
after 1945. I hated
Hitler, too. But I loved
my Hitler stamp.

I loved taking him out
of the wax-paper sleeve
in my stamp collecting book
and holding him in my hand

under the light. And what
would my father have said if he knew
I was up there in my room
under his roof, hoarding Hitler,

harboring Hitler, holding Hitler up
to the light?

Sunday School

The slow boy wants to know
if God, too, is slow.
Spitballs fill the air.
A few land in his hair
and stick there like burrs
while others glance wetly
off his cheek and fall
to the floor like crumpled
prayers. Very slowly
he raises the splayed
white flag of his hand,
but the teacher goes on
writing the long answer
up on the blackboard
with her back to the class,
and the children are reloading
the empty barrels of their pens.

Staring at the Blind

My eyes are the flies,
your eyes are the spilled
milk. You are the cow
whose tail the farmer cut off—
defenseless now against the flies
which keep returning to feed
on the spilled white milk
of your blind eyes. "Let us pray,"
says the amazingly graceless
born-again Christian sitting
next to you on the train. "Let us
ask God, together, to restore
the sight to your eyes." Your eyes
are the guinea pigs, this guy is
a pig farmer from hell, trying
to cross-breed his faith with
your life story. I want to
cut his praying hands off.
I want to open his eyes
to your eyes. Your eyes are
the bees, hovering, oscillating,
making something perfectly rich
and amazing on the inside,
something heavy and thick with
mystery, which some meddling hands
would unburden the bees of.
But the bees need no unburdening.

Song

A suicide bomber isn't born a suicide bomber.
He wasn't a suicide bomber in elementary school
when he drew a spiky, yellow, exploding sun

above a little town between two green hills
and gave it to the teacher, and the teacher smiled.
On the day the suicide bomber was born

his father danced through the market from stall
to stall, singing the good news out until
the spiky, yellow, exploding sun went down

over the little town, and by then all the people
in the houses huddled between two green hills
had heard of the birth of the suicide bomber

who wasn't a suicide bomber at all, at all.
He was never in his life what you would call
a suicide bomber. He was his father's son

till that day in the market, the people and animals
splattering like so many fruits and vegetables....
That was the day the suicide bomber was born.
An exploding sun. Like millions of exploding suns.

Malala

Teach the women this and only this
We have killed each other over the women
We have killed ourselves over the women
We have killed the women because the women
are so beautiful we want to die

We must save the women from themselves
We must save ourselves from the women
Teach the women this and only this
They are so beautiful we want to die
We must save them for ourselves only
ourselves only ourselves only

Laconic

He sounds so far away. He could be
in Sparta, where terseness of speech
was a matter of reputation. But he's only
in his teens where his reputation
is a matter of life and death. And he doesn't
need a coat. And especially not a raincoat.
Because the elements don't affect him.
Because he's impervious to rain and cold.
Because the weather rolls off him like
requests to lift the seat, put back
the milk, how was school today, do
tell. And his voice, on the rare occasion
that it pokes out of the gravelly
tunnel of his throat, sounds deeper and
a lot more distant, though it barely
clears the sill of his lips with a single syllable,
a vowel that passes for a greeting
when he passes with a grunt. So far away,
he could be underwater, the vowels bubbling up
so that it looks to the alarmed observer
like he's drowning. But he's singing.
He likes it down there where you can't
reach him unless you're willing to jump in
yourself. And he knows you aren't willing.
And he knows he's safe. It may seem cold
to you, but to him the water is warm. He may
stay in for a few more years. When he comes out
he'll be older in ways that will be hard
to put the wrinkled tips of his fingers on.

Daylight

In the dream my son is a little boy again,
and it feels like daylight savings time
in the fall, when we all fall back. It's a bit
of an adjustment getting used to his
little body again, which he had just
finished growing out of. Home from
college now, he's a toddler again (it
makes sense in the dream) so we have to
adjust all the clocks. And it feels
strange picking him up and carrying him
on one hip, and then the other, changing
position like that, feeling his small bones
on my big bones again. I ask him if
he pooped, because it's our shared business
again. And I can't help wondering at
the change, the imposition, like a curfew, though
it's no imposition in the dream—I love it,
I welcome it, like a time change in the spring
when there's more time and there's more
light, and it feels like the world is growing
young again, though really it's just as old
as ever, and growing older, and darker all the time.

AA

We'll drink
the day
we think
we're cured.

The day
we kick
we're cured.
Till then

we kick
the bot-
tle, then
we drag

the butt
to meetings.
A drag!
First things

first. Meetings
get better.
First thing
we know

we're better.
Got hope.
Now we
got feelings.

We hope
we never
get feeling
too good.

We never
remember
too good
all the pain.

Remember,
we buried
all the pain,
but good.

When we're buried
they'll plug
our butt
in the ground.

We'll unplug
the jug then.
We'll have grounds.
We'll be cured.

The Procedure

He only read for pleasure anymore.
So when the pain got bad
and he had to go to the hospital
for a procedure whose name
wasn't in his dictionary

because his dictionary was older
than his procedure and older
than his reading pleasure
and much, much older
than his doctor who looked
to be all of twenty-three,

he plopped himself down
in a waiting-room chair
and read. He was reading a novel
that he'd read before, and since
he only read for pleasure anymore
he was reading it again
and smiling with pleasure when

the nurse called him in.
He thought she resembled
the young and pretty ingenue
who was the brave protagonist
in the fiction he was still hugging
to his chest an hour later

like a small pillow,
when the brusque and bearded
anesthesiologist, who resembled
the antagonist looking for a good
vein, tried and failed and tried
and failed again to pry it
from his gentle reader's hand.

Stealing Band-Aids from Hospitals

A kind of Robin Hood
taking from the health care industry
and giving to the little guy, the little
fingers, the little paper cuts and dry cracked hands
that needed to be covered. A kind of
John Henry going up against the steam engine
of the mega-hospitals,
marching into those waiting rooms
and turning off the televisions. A kind of
Johnny Appleseed turning off televisions
wherever he went, for the benefit of everyone,
especially the future generations.
And when they called out his name
in those hospital waiting rooms,
he was a kind of John Doe,
a kind of John Q. Public following the nurse
into the little examining room
and waiting there all alone with his body
and his backpack
for an eternity for the doctor to come—
plenty of time for appropriating
lots of band-aids and tongue depressors
and rolls of surgical tape and gauze,
and maybe, come to think of it, some of these
elusive little boxes of tissues
that one always finds in hospitals,
for the little guy
who can never seem to find them
when he needs them.

Aubade

The sun is raising its hand again—
it's practically levitating in its seat,
reaching its fingers up as high as they will go,
spreading them, wiggling them, stretching
and straining its toes and kicking out its feet,
exploding with *oh, oh, oh, I know, I know, I know.*
It's dying—the sun is simply dying—to get the earth's
attention. But the earth turns an infinitely
patient, sardonically tilted, patronizing eye
toward the sun, and the birds juke and jeer,
and the trees bend over backwards with
laughter. And what can the people do
but get up, urinate, roll their eyes and yawn
at the sun's same old wrong answer.

Elbow

My blind friend wants to know if the girl he's seeing
is good-looking. On a scale of one to ten.
So I tell him about the lioness at the zoo,
how I stood in front of her cage and just stared
for hours—all afternoon—until the people
with their cameras and children and balloons
and zoo-fact coloring books had all gone home,
all gone home. And still I couldn't see it.

"Couldn't see what?" he asks, tilting his head
and staring at the infinity over my shoulder,
and seeing there only beauty on a scale of
one to ten. "The terror," I tell him. "Terror on the scale of
dinosaurs. Volcanoes. Planetary terror. Terror that would
destroy you if it didn't live in ten square feet, in a zoo."

"That's dark," he says, and blinks twice.
Then he tilts his head the other way and asks
about the size of her breasts. "I haven't actually
touched them yet," he says, "except once,
and that was only accidentally with my elbow
when I was showing her how to guide me through doors."

Bobby Bro

The real names are so much sexier.
And the innocent don't need protecting
now that they're in their sixties, clean
and sober, their mothers dead or demented.
So Bobby Bro was his real name.
He should have been a famous quarterback
with a name like that. A movie star,
prizefighter, golf pro, lead singer, lead
scorer. He was sexy and ragged and scored
with the hottest girls in my high school
mostly because, without fail, he could score
weed. Which is what he was most famous for.

He wore a silver hemostat on a gold chain
around his neck. It caught the light and winked
as he twisted his torso in the passenger seat
of my mother's car, turning to take the roach
from the hand passing it up from the backseat.
With the manual dexterity of a surgeon
he disengaged the hemostat's locking mechanism,
eyed the tip narrowly, clamped the roach
perpendicular to its axis (like a blood vessel
or a fallopian tube awaiting ligation),
raised it up to an almost imperceptible
flaxen mustache and sucked vigorously,

surrendering it to me with popping eyes,
farting lips, inflated cheeks. As for my mother,
she never met Bobby Bro nor heard his real name
uttered. Because I always invented an alias,
a poor substitute, a travesty really, as I made up
my alibis for where I was going and what

I was doing with her car, which I returned
with all the windows down, after smoking the requisite
ratifying bone to seal the sale
with Bobby Bro and his great and good name.

Dueling Banjos

He was a fingerpicker, and I was a frailer,
and she was this beautiful dark-haired guitar
with this forthright mischief in her eyes,
this clef tattooed above her sacrum,
this mother-of-pearl shiver she sent up

my fifteen-year-old spine. I was in love with her,
me, a masturbator in God's eyes as I locked
the door, closed my eyes, and my mouth
sang mute accompaniment to my own flailing
hand: traditional enough, but back then

I thought I'd go blind if I kept it up. Then Doc
Watson came to town with that happy guileless
Tennessee voice, that flatpicking style as clean
as a ringing bell, and his son Merle on banjo.
We both bought tickets and asked her to go.

You know how this story ends. She goes with him,
the fingerpicker. And I can't stop crying.
And I can't stop frailing. And six months later
Merle dies in a tragic tractor accident,
and Doc stops singing for a long, long time.

Poem Beginning with a Last Line
from *Dubliners*

In my heart I had always despised him a little.
He was very well read, hopelessly intelligent,
soulless. For example, he would probably
recognize the line, and the story it's borrowed from—
"stolen from," he would say—but he wouldn't get
the poem. Which is why I feel compelled to write it.
We were both English majors at an obscure little
liberal arts college that catered to creative fuck-ups
on the Hudson. I'd read a little Joyce in high school.
He said he'd read *all* of Joyce, including *Finnegan's Wake*
twice, and a biography of Nora Barnacle, which
"helps explain Joyce's scatological bent," he said.
His girlfriend and my girlfriend shared the same first name,
only spelled differently. He said he'd done *everything*
with her, including some things he said I couldn't imagine.
I said I was pretty sure I'd already imagined everything
one could do with a girl. That's when he gave me
his shit-eating grin, lit his pipe which had gone out
in the meantime, sucked on it vigorously until
a cloud of brownish smoke subsumed his head and most of
the upper half of his body. "Not this, you haven't,"
he said. Then he told me things that both disgusted
and aroused me. They disgusted me first, then aroused
me later after going over and over them in a kind of
holding pattern in my head. I wavered about whether
to tell my girlfriend, judging not to in the end. Thus
she remained innocent of it, as though I'd changed
her name, to protect her, the way they do in novels.
Her name was Melodie, spelled that way and not the other.

The Cat Is Sleeping on a Draft of This Poem

that doesn't have a cat in it
though it does have
some children and some dogs
and some old ideas about the world
as it was.
As it is, the cat has no idea—
she simply padded over to the page
where she sensed some center was
or had been
or would be again
and without insinuating herself
and without inserting herself
she sat on it
and like an onset
of warm summer rain
started washing herself
with the darting pink washcloth
of her tongue impinging
on every square inch
of the field, every grass blade
every tree-branch, leaf, mailbox, huddled house
and all the old ideas
which are getting warmer
getting warmer
and also the children and the dogs
who just kept running and playing together
as if they would remain
children and dogs forever.

Rewind

The homeless are giving their money
to poor you and me, stalled here
in traffic, waiting to get home
to the lost and hopeless suburbs.

They're reaching into their little cups
and giving away whatever
their fingers happen to touch first,
and without thinking twice.

The clouds are passing weirdly overhead
as you and I roll down our windows
and look directly into the faces
of our backing-away benefactors

whose eyes are rolling counterclockwise,
and the balked and steaming traffic
backs up all the way into the obscure
streets of the impoverished heart.

Mary Dyer

I'm sitting in the Dunkin' Donuts on Beacon Street
across from the statue of Mary Dyer, Quaker, witness
for religious freedom, hanged on Boston Common
in 1660. Her face is slightly averted, slanting
downward, as though it were raining out. She has
that drenched stare that certain statues have. She's wearing
a hat, a sort of bonnet, very plain, perhaps for religious
reasons—covering her head before God. And the girl
behind the counter at Dunkin' Donuts is wearing a headscarf.
I think she's Muslim. She's very attractive. And when
she was taking my order, she glanced over my shoulder
at the statue of Mary Dyer across the street. And when
she delicately handed me my medium regular, her eyes
flitted back to the statue of Mary Dyer, alighting there like two
gray doves. And finally when she gave me my change
I said thank you and tried to catch her eye, but she just
looked down, then away, then back at Mary Dyer as though
the two of them were communing. So I'm wondering
if this attractive Muslim girl in the headscarf is thinking
about death. Or even suicide. Because I googled Mary Dyer
on my iPhone, and it says she *wanted* to die. It says
she was convicted by the Puritans of being a Quaker,
not once but twice, and spared both times. They banished her
to Rhode Island. But she returned to Massachusetts, openly
defying the anti-Quaker laws. On the gallows they gave her
one last chance to repent. She refused. And she was hanged
and died a martyr. And now the girl in the headscarf is laughing
with her colleague, a handsome young man with perfect teeth
and flawless skin, as he bears a tray of donuts aloft,
high above their heads. And life is good. And life is sweet.
And Mary Dyer across the street has a perfectly drenched look,
a verdigris look, like the Statue of Liberty, only smaller,
and seated, and with both hands resting quietly in her lap.

Unrequited

Whenever she ate she talked about food,
all the unforgettable meals of her past,
with her mouth full. And he'd listen
as the food in her mouth grew smaller
and smaller and more insignificant with each
description of some towering feast or
peerless confection of her youth. Squinting
with pleasure at all those distant pleasures,
she'd shake her lovely head as if to say: Pity,
you can't quite see them from here. And he'd look
down at his plate, then across at her lovely head
and yearn for her eyes, which were elsewhere;
for her lips and teeth and tongue, which were
elsewhere too. And take her hands, like crumbs.

Rebound Banjo

She left him for her ex
who played the 5-string banjo
in a bluegrass band and whom
she'd left for him—and not
three months before—for a short

sweet-smelling spring,
wound him like a string around
the tuning peg of her index,
touched him and he stiffened,
and he sang. And he broke

down and wept when she went back
to her banjo-playing ex
like a second thought about
a second fiddle, a repeating
chorus or refrain. So he went out west

to forget her. But he couldn't forget—
he saw her everywhere, saw her hands
in the hands of strangers, saw her hair
on the heads of strangers, saw her breasts
in the shapes of the Grand Tetons

high against the big Wyoming sky
at twilight. And on a side street
in Jackson, he saw it in the window
of the pawn shop, its slender neck adorned
with mother-of-pearl inlay,

its fifth tuning peg indented like
a new paragraph, a new chapter,
its pale full-moon face a blank
slate. And he bought it for fifty bucks
which included the case, capo, strap, three

fingerpicks and a Mel Bay's *Learn to Play the Five-String Banjo* book. He was motivated. To win her back, of course. And of course he didn't win her back. But he did learn to play in a frailing way

"Cripple Creek" and "Old Joe Clark"
and "Sail Away Ladies Sail Away."

The Bad Guys

Have you noticed
how the little boys
and the retired generals
both like to talk about the bad guys?
It's as though they were talking to each other.
Maybe they *are* talking to each other.
Maybe the little boys are advising
the retired generals
on how to advise the military,
the Congress, the President who is also
(have you noticed?) talking about
the bad guys. Who are the bad guys anyway?
That's what I'd like to know.
Maybe they're the ones who don't love us,
says one of the little boys.
Or don't love us the way
we want them to love us. They love
to hate us, says a retired general.
Which is a very tough kind of love
to carry in your heart, adds the President,
speaking softly to the little boys.
The Dalai Lama and the Pope and the retired
librarian who lives next door all say
we should simply try to love the bad guys,
I say. If all we do is love the bad guys
they will kill us all, says another retired
general. Not if we tell their mothers first,
says one of the little boys. We can't just go
and tell their mothers, says a congressman.
Why can't we? says the retired
librarian standing next to me at attention.

Because you have already
killed our mothers, says a bad guy
who has somehow snuck in
disguised as a little boy,
and he detonates
and we all fall down.

II.

My Underpants

I found them on the bathroom floor
after my cousin and her boyfriend
left for Ithaca. They were green
with gold stripes and they weren't
mine. I stood there for a long time
considering them. They weren't
dirty but they weren't exactly clean
either. They were unwashed.
But they weren't unclean the way
a dead bird is unclean, or the way
an unsanctified thing or an unholy thing
is unclean. I picked them up, and did I
smell them? I want to say I smelled them.
I may have smelled them because
they weren't unclean and they were undoubtedly
my cousin's boyfriend's and he is a good man,
not a holy man but a good man with a good
job in Ithaca, New York, and an excellent beard.
Of course I thought about returning them,
sending them back in a mailer or small brown box,
and I thought about washing them,
though they weren't mine and they weren't
unclean, only unwashed, and they weren't
sexy, only colorful. They were more colorful
than all of my underpants put together.
You will want to know I am wearing them
as I write this. Much time has elapsed
since that day in the bathroom. My cousin
and her boyfriend have gotten married.
I have gotten married myself. My wife
has no idea about the provenance
of the green underpants. She thinks they are mine.
She washes them with my underpants

and her underpants, and she puts them all
in a sweet-smelling pile on top of the dresser.
I think there is something a little holy
about a pile of clean underpants on top of a dresser.
I think that putting them away in a drawer
would be like putting your light under a bushel,
or like locking a bird up in a cage,
or like packing up a good green thing
in a small brown box
and sending it far, far away from you.

The Only Question

She was very beautiful.
Exceptionally beautiful.
Beautiful in the way of
certain sudden realizations,
like: My god, is it raining?
or: Look how huge the moon!

She was at the poetry reading.
My poetry reading. Just one among
many pretty undergraduates
until the Q&A. That was when
she raised her hand in the third row
and asked me: "What inspires you?"

What I should have said was:
"Beauty. Beauty inspires me."
And left it at that. And let
the awkward silence speak
for itself while I stared at her
from up at the podium for perhaps

a whole minute, ignoring
the chair of the English Department
clearing his throat, the few diffuse
titters filling the room, the enormous
moon filling the big picture
window as my drenched gaze

fell on her, steadily, like a fine summer
rain falling on the second seat
in the third row. But what I said
a little dryly, was: "Literature. Great
literature inspires me." And she looked
away. And hers was the only question.

Disbelief

Take this beautiful woman
in my arms. I don't
believe my eyes. And I don't
believe my arms. I don't
believe my ears when she says
she loves me too.
Time passes like you
wouldn't believe. I think
I'm happy. Then I think
I'm sad. Then happy again.
Then not. I don't
believe my thoughts,
nor anything the past
has taught—not one
belief I ever learned before
from anything. I lay aside
all thoughts of what I am
and what love is. It's not
that I believe in nothing,
if that's what you're thinking.
I believe in disbelief. I believe
you can walk through this world
and not believe it for a minute.
You can get to the end of it
and not believe that either.
You can sit in a small room
all alone with your body,
don the humble hospital gown
that closes in the back,
and when the doctor comes in
with his numbers,

which are your numbers,
you can not believe them either.
You can let them fall from his lips,
skim your ears,
pool on the floor where his eyes
and your eyes have fallen.

A Night at the Opera

I took my son and daughter to *Don Giovanni*
when they were six and four and two hundred and three
respectively. What was I thinking?
I was recently separated from their mother
who had no ear for opera and no love in her heart
for me. But I loved Mozart and I loved
my children, and it seemed a good idea at the time.
It was an "amateur" production, from the Latin
amare: to love. And it was during my "visitation,"
from *visitare:* to visit. "It sounds like
you and Mommy screaming at each other,"
said my son after the first duet: "*Non sperar
se non m'uccidi*" ("Do not hope unless
you kill me"). We left before the abject last act
when the visitation of the murdered Commendatore
drags Don Giovanni down to hell with him
surrounded by hellfire and a chorus of demons. By then
my kids were fast asleep, and I had to half drag, half
carry them, one on each hip, down the aisle and out
the door to the street. I paused in the cool night air
to regroup, revise, redistribute the weight
of my sleeping cargo, jettison the ex and the demons
and all the dead weight of that dead marriage, tell Mozart
to take a backseat to my daughter gently snoring
in my arms now and my son riding piggyback
as I carried them like that, a kind of armor,
their sweet sleep-smell enclosing me
all the way back to my car.

Tenth Grade Vocabulary List

I put them all in alphabetical order—
apposite, betwixt, crenellated, duenna,
etcetera—on 8 x 5 index cards,
with their definitions on the back
in etymological order, and studied them
all alone in my room. But in order
to own them, to internalize them,
to be able to retrieve them at the drop
of a word, I knew I needed to use them,
to say them, to embed them in
my sentences. "Please pass the friable,
crenellated chicken pot pie betwixt
the sweet potatoes and green beans,
duenna," I said to my mother
at dinner. She looked over her shoulder
and winced, as though I'd fired a volley
of vocabulary over her head, nicking
her earlobe, embedding itself in the wall
like shrapnel. There's no getting around it,
the big words are intimidating, formidable,
redoubtable, apposite and sometimes
the opposite of apposite. But a hairless,
feckless, rangy kid who didn't know
how to fight, and didn't have a girlfriend,
could use them to good advantage,
to parley, and to parlay, and at parties
to impress girls, blow his rivals away.

Lloyd

I had a friend named Lloyd when I was eight.
I will always remember Lloyd for his two l's
which came at the beginning. I didn't know
much. But I knew two l's could come at the beginning
already at the tender age of eight. Life went
on. I learned about llamas. And Prince Llewellyn.
And the Iliad, which doesn't have two l's
at the beginning, though it kind of looks like it does.
And eventually I lost touch with Lloyd although
I never forgot him. Because every single unlikely
superfluous thing, every odd doubling or identical
twin at the beginning of anything, reminds me of Lloyd
and his two l's: the first one loud, capital, rushing
in, the second one silent, reticent, redundant as Lloyd himself.

Thrombosis Trombone

Two twins appeared in my sixth grade class
the year my father had his coronary
thrombosis. I couldn't tell them apart until
I got to know them better on the inside,
and then the resemblance all but disappeared. One
played bassoon, the other played timpani
in our grade school band. We squeaked and sawed
two concerts out that year, one in the fall
and one in the spring. I played the trombone,
which has a spit-valve for cleaning out obstructions
accreting on the inside. My father lay down
on the kitchen floor, his mouth working noiselessly
like a greased hinge. It comes from the Greek word
meaning lump, or clump, or curd, or clot
of milk. Spit-valves can get clogged up with
spit, or gum, or snot, or even a deciduous
tooth. What I felt on the inside was
less sadness than anger. And then a kind of
shame. I couldn't see my mother but I knew
she was sitting out there in the dark auditorium
all alone. I emptied my spit-valve onto the head
of the self-important first trumpet sitting
in front of me on the penultimate concert riser. One
of the twins saw me do it. The timpani twin.
Our eyes met and he looked away. But I knew
he was laughing hysterically on the inside.

Works for Trumpet

We are listening to Alison Balsom
play Bach. "Do we have to

listen to this?" Amber, eleven,
buckled up in the passenger seat,

balks, bucks. We're late for school—
her backpack, lunchbox, and violin

ride mutely in the back. She looks
down at the CD box, makes a face:

"Who is *Botch,* anyway?"
Her violin leaps violently to the floor

as I brake for a stopped school bus.
"It's not *Botch,*" I tell her. "It's *Bach*—

only the greatest musician who ever lived,
that's who." She gives the box a second,

closer look—"Bach is pretty. How old is Bach?"—
frowning at the photo of Alison Balsom

on the cover. "That's not Bach," I tell her.
"It's Alison Balsom. On trumpet. And yes,

she *is* pretty." Amber raises her left eyebrow,
then stitches it to its twin. "A *girl*

playing the trumpet?" And I can hear
the wheels turning, tuning, inside her head

as the school bus trundles dumbly along
and I follow close behind. "There aren't

any girls who play trumpet in *my* school.
Only boys." And Alison belts out another

string of impossibly gorgeous arpeggios.
And Amber looks out the window, scratches

her head. She is listening. I don't say
a word, pull in behind the school bus, park,

and we sit there for a long time, the violin
on the floor, the trumpet in the air, Alison

Balsom breathing Bach, breathing beauty,
Amber late for school and listening hard.

Historical Clock

Don't you just want to dummy slap history?
Don't you want to knock some sense
into the fourteenth century, tell them about the rats
and the fleas, bacteriology, sanitation, personal
hygiene? I mean wouldn't you just love
to bitch slap those peasants and popes
who blamed the bubonic plague on the Jews,
those flagellants who blamed it on themselves,
those doctors with their humors and bloodletting
and leeches? And aren't your fingers just itching
to box the ears of Europe in the late middle ages
for its Inquisitions, its tribunals, its autos-da-fé?
All those poor apostates, heretics, bigamists, sodomizers
who were just like you and me. Just like you and me.
For their sake—for all our sakes—I say,
let's clock history, cuff it upside the head,
for all its ignorance, sanctimony, rectitude.

Spiritual Mom

Mom got spiritual in her late fifties,
and we really had no patience for all
the forgiveness. It was disconcerting
the way she'd kneel down on the floor
in the middle of the conversation
and hug the dog, whispering affirmations
into its long ear, stroking and folding it
inside out like a pocket. When she emptied
her bank account and gave all the money
to whoever asked, wandering around downtown,
reaching into her purse to offer whatever
her fingers touched first, it was the last
straw. We did an intervention, as they call it
in the field of addiction. We sat her down
and confronted her on her spiritual habit.
The room grew quiet as Mom wept softly,
her eyes searching the floor for what to say.
The silence was terrible—even the dog
cocked its head in that doglike listening way
for some kind of affirmation that Mom
had heard us, and understood, and would cease
her spiritual ways, or at least be in the world
a little more and no longer walking around like
she didn't have a colon, with one foot in Heaven
and an ear to the hot little mouth of God.

The Meteorologist's Breasts

which are right next to the hurricane
which is inching up the East Coast
are lovely and on the small side.
The hurricane is predicted to be
the biggest to hit the East Coast
since they started naming hurricanes
in 1953. *Love is greater than fear*
said the bumper sticker on the truck
in front of me in traffic. It took
three and a half hours to get home.
Her blouse is soft and blue and stretchy.
When I lose power she goes on pointing
to Atlantic City, smiling bravely.

October

Everyone called him Toby
but his real name was October,
but nobody knew that except the teacher
who assured him his secret was safe with her.
That first day in September, he arrived
early, before all the other students,
and introduced himself to her
and told her about his hippie parents
who had named him October
because they loved October
and because they got married in October,
and so a year later in October
he was born October. She said
she thought it was a lovely name and a lovely
story. But he said no, it was an affliction.
He said the kids in his old school
called him Ock. Or else they called him Brr.
They made fun of him in cruel ways,
like rubbing their arms and stamping their feet
whenever he passed them in the hall:
"Brr, it's cold in here," they said.
And they teased him about June,
the bookish girl with pimples and thick glasses,
saying lewd things like: "It feels like October
in June." It got so bad he had to move away
and start life over. His hippie father
put in for a transfer. His mother who did macramé
could do macramé anywhere. So they moved
here. And he started life anew, with a new
name, a new identity. It was not unlike
the federal witness protection program,
and his parents were guilty as hell
and were never prosecuted.

Dear Edvard Munch

We love a good scream.
And we'd like to put yours
to music with a video
option (contract enclosed).
Pain is in, especially pain in
tune, and the gravelly voice
of our own wretchedness
broadcast back to us
is beautiful to our modern
way of thinking. We were thinking
Joe Cocker, or maybe Springsteen,
Tina Turner if the figure on the bridge
is female (please advise). The baldness
is brilliant, Edvard, brilliant—
baldness is in, and we love it
as much as we love the bloody sky,
the oozing lake and rolling precipice
(blood and ooze and rock and roll
are in) and we would only lower
one hand (the irony will not be lost
on the grandmothers) and it could be
either hand—your choice—the other
remaining at the ear the way you have it—
and lo! the scream turns into
song, the sexless figure turns
into the sexy recording artist
with a hand cupped to one ear,
the mouth unchanged in the center,
like the eye of the cyclone
which is raging all around in a black
chorus. Sign in the lower
right-hand corner
and fed-ex back to us.

Gauguin's Grandson

was named Paul Gauguin,
too. He was an artist,
too. He lived in Denmark
in his grandfather's shadow
all his life. And he chafed
against that shadow.
Like living under a rock—
a rock as big as the biggest
island in French Polynesia.
He painted only insects.
Insects that live under rocks—
beetles, ants, centipedes,
pill bugs. In a later period,
he painted only his wife Marta
in only her long black hair
and horn-rimmed glasses.
Toward the end of his life
he made hundreds of collages
of orthopterous insects—
katydids, mantids, cicadas,
crickets and grasshoppers
with long hind legs for jumping
or, you could say, flying;
and for making a rasping, chafing
sound or, you could say, song.

Juvenilia

Those early poems I wrote,
the ones that rhymed and smote
whatever needed smiting in the world
of the poem, how they puff themselves up!

It's not that juvenilia and genitalia
rhyme a little, but more that such a little thing
should dare to dream so big: "A King's Lament
to His Kidnapped Nubian Concubine,"

with an India ink illustration of a dragon,
would surely win Cheryl Spiata's attention,
or so I thought. But I never dreamed
her attention would morph into a kind of

mountaintop in my head where the muses live
forever—still decades after losing touch with her
and everyone else in that kingdom. I was smitten
by poetry early. And I've been edging toward it

and away ever since. It's a double-edged sword
that, as Emily Dickinson said, makes you feel
physically as if the top of your head
were taken off; but, as Auden said, makes

nothing happen. So it breaks your heart twice:
first by piercing it, then by being thinner
than paper. Thinner even than air. So it makes no
shadow in the world. Barely an echo.

The Emperor's New Clothes

I stole a bathmat
from the Royal Copenhagen Hotel

because it said *Royal Copenhagen* on it
and how cool is that

for stepping out of your shower onto
every day of your life in America

as a souvenir
of a few dissolute days in Denmark?

I like to snuggle the rich velvety pile
with my ten poor stubby toes

while I'm still dripping from the shower,
where I get all my best ideas—

then I feel a little like Søren Kierkegaard,
and a little like King Frederick,

and a little like Hans Christian Andersen
getting out of his claw-foot tub

and getting a great idea,
and standing there for a few timeless

dripping moments,
then rushing to his writing table

and spinning the yarn, still naked,
in one inspired sitting,

his trail of wet footprints disappearing
before the ink had dried.

Conversations with My Son

Pretty amazing
that I can think of you
and tell you so with my thumbs
and seconds later
that thought reaches you.

duh dad its the 21st centry in
case u havnt notcd

Oh, I've noticed. And would it be
too much to ask
for us to talk on the telephone
sometime later this afternoon
or this evening?

i cant theres a game tonite
and rite now im pregaming

What does "pre-gaming" mean?

dad u dont hv to punctuate evrything

(http://www.urbandictionary.com/
define.pre-gaming:
pre-gaming—drinking several
alcoholic beverages
or using illegal drugs
before going to a larger function
in preparation of getting toasted)

So what else are you learning
up there in college
at fifty grand a year???

um
i guess im expanding
my vocabulary dad
and yours :)

U-Haul

I was glad to. After all,
it would be just him and me in the cab
together for eight whole hours,
talking. He'd been away at college
for four whole years, text-messaging
every now and then, and now
I expected some full sentences.
That was the deal. In return
we'd use my credit card and I would drive
him and all his worldly possessions
home. Somewhere around Delaware
the mirror on the passenger side
starting turning inward against the wind
and I couldn't see, and it wouldn't
stay when we opened the window
and readjusted it. I told him
to take off his shoes and give me his laces,
and I'd pull over and tie the mirror
to the antenna to keep it from drifting.
He asked me why his shoes and not
my shoes? It was a good question,
the kind of question you might debate
in a sociology class in college
if you were still in college. But we were
speeding down I-95 in a U-Haul
with one functioning mirror, a resourceful
father at the wheel, a credit card
in his pocket, his thumbs keeping time
to an old-fashioned song in his head
that only he could hear, and a son
drowning out that song now, turning
the radio on. Loud. Louder. Silently
bending down to untie his shoes.

Looking for Something Dead
to Roll Around In

Feeling surly and misanthropic on Thanksgiving,
I excused myself from the table
where the gratitude was so thick you could
rip it with your canines, tear it clean off the bone
and carry it dangling and bloody in your teeth
right out of the room.
                        Then I sniffed around
in an adjacent room for a while and, finding a dead
poet on one of the bookshelves, buried myself
in some sweetly decaying, quaintly boxy poems
for several pages, exulting in the faintly
mildewing historical smell, before you suddenly
burst into the room and yelled at me to stop
stewing.

The Good Fight

Which one
is the good fight
anyway?
Isn't it the good guy
kicking butt but
a little reluctantly
because he's good
and hates to have to?
And since no one else would
and the wrong would just
go on unrighted,
he steps up to the plate
and takes a few good swings
and puts that baby to bed? Go
fuck yourself, you said,
and have said nothing else
all day. Now it's night
and your silence is still
that choked, caked, kill-
all-the-motherfuckers-take-
no-prisoners kind
you have honed to a fine
squint. But I only
meant to point out
what was wrong—to right it.
I don't know much,
but I know I love
your butt more than God
or country. And when we fight,
it hurts me right
here—right here.

And now I think
the good fight is the one
we get through
quickly, get to the other side of
with nothing dead or otherwise
irreparable floating
in the churning reddish
air we part like a sea,
miraculously
finding our way back
to each other's
arms.

Defense Secretary Slips on Ice

I bet he didn't
see that one coming.
Invisible enemy.
Crushed the phalanx
of his little finger
trying to break his fall
on his own front steps,
rushing out the door this morning
to the big meeting,
a big black-and-blue mark
blooming on his bum now.
The newspapers aren't saying
anything about his bum,
but I bet it hurts like hell to sit
down at the peace table.
He's probably wincing right now.
Which may be why
we're all still at war.
Another beautiful fall
morning. Cold and wet,
the air full of the crisp,
exquisite smells of death.

Dooley for State Rep

A small band of supporters
holding up signs and waving
on the corner of Pleasant and Main
on this gelid November morning—and who
is Dooley? He's the one among them
who isn't wearing a hat, the one
with the gelled hair, very red
ears, frozen smile, waving at me
as I drive by, the wind chill
minus twenty, his breath sending out
these little diplomatic envoys
of wispy white warmth every which way.
This man without the hat, without
the sense to put on a hat in weather
like this, this man who wants my vote,
who wants to represent me in the capital,
this man who made the bad decision
to forgo the hat this morning because
it would cover his excellent hair,
or it would make him look weak
when he needs to look strong,
needs to look excellent, and I think
this is exactly what's wrong with America
and its leaders and its image in the eyes
of the world: it all comes down to this
hat, which this man who wants my vote,
but shall not have it, doesn't have on.

The Republicans

So random the way it touched down
when we were sitting there talking about
the Republicans. You said: *I stand
corrected.* And that pause opened up
like the brief, warm, unstable condition
ahead of a cold front, the kind that spawns
tornadoes. And inside of that pause your stuffy
I stand corrected stood there stiffly
ridiculous and resonating in the itchy
combustible air between us, and it was so
random. It was so ordinary, like opening
a window, and then another, the way my eyes
widened and your eyes widened in sympathy
like a mutual last gasp before it hit us
and we burst into uncontrollable and inexorable
and exorbitant laughter, violently rotating
between us and around us and inside us,
churning and merciless and devastating,
wreaking havoc with my respiratory system
and your respiratory system, so we couldn't
breathe and we couldn't talk and my face hurt
and my lungs hurt and my head hurt and my jaw—
and just when I thought it was over I looked up
and saw another one coming.

Precedent

She sued him over his sonnet
for libel. Because he used her real name
in that poem about the good old days
when she was bad and beautiful. He went
into such poetic detail in the second half
of the octave, that the reader feels a sweet
gasp in the loins to read it. "Your Honor,
I am honored," he declared (it was quite the turn)
"to be sued over my sonnet. May it set
a precedent. May it get people reading
sonnets again!" Then he argued that it praised
rather than defamed her, that if read properly
she was its heroine, and that though he published it
in a magazine, they never paid him a cent.

Bust

The summer I was 16,
which came on the heels
of the spring that I was 16,
which came in the middle

of my 16-year-old body
like the sweetest of all
pollen counts, Faith Roffman
unbuttoned her blouse

and let me see her breasts,
and also let me touch them,
and kiss them, and suck them.
She was much older, nearly

18, and it was a short
spring that summer, and then
she left for college and I never
saw her or her breasts again.

But that fall our class took a field trip
to the museum, and there among
the busts of the Greek and Roman
gods I saw Faith's breasts—I swear

to God. They were hers. I mean,
I should know. I mean, I knew
their shape by heart, and lo—
there they were on display

for the whole world to see, plain
as the nose on my face, which
I was just dying to bury between
those breasts impersonating the breasts

of Faith Roffman. But our history
teacher herded us into the next gallery.
And it was full of Egyptian sarcophagi
which looked a lot like bathtubs,

though really they were coffins.

Collage

All of the art students' hairdos hold together: a newspaper hat, a pencil barrette,
a paintbrush, the weather, gravity, glue.
Art students hold that the nude is not—
gravity is—what moves us and holds us
glued to her breasts. Her skin is the weather.
That triangle of hair is a newspaper hat
penciled in and folded over, holding together.
Under the moon and a newspaper hat,
I make love to a blue-haired student of art
with pencil-breasts, a single paintbrush
miraculously holding all that weather of hair.

The Things I Want to Say

I like to ask people the way
to places I know how to get to already.
It helps me hear better
the things they're not saying

which are the things I want to say.
It's hard to put into words exactly,
is what their faces seem to convey
as they look around thoughtfully,

searchingly, that faraway look in their eyes
(which is exactly what I'm looking for)
getting closer, getting warmer,
as their hands begin to describe

tiny circles in air, building bridges,
cutting corners, hands which have already
been there and back many times

in the saying.

Acknowledgments

Thanks to the following publications in which many of these poems, sometimes in earlier versions, originally appeared:

American Poetry Journal, Blueline, Bluestem, Caesura, Coachella Review, Coe Review, Comstock Review, Dead Snakes, Earth's Daughters, The Entroper, Evening Street Review, Five Quarterly, The 5-2 Crime Poetry Weekly, Houseboat, Ibbetson Street, IthacaLit, Kansas City Voices, Kentucky Review, The Linnet's Wings, Loch Raven Review, Mad Swirl, Malala: Poems for Malala Yousafzai, Miller's Pond, Mud Season Review, Negative Suck, Off the Coast, Poets Online, Red Booth Review, Seems, Shortpoem.org, Snail Mail Review, Spillway, Switched-on Gutenberg, Tar River Poetry, Toasted Cheese Literary Journal, Umbrella: A Journal of Poetry, Universal Table, Weird Cookies, Wordgathering

Cover art by Christine O'Reilly; cover art photo and author photo by Jonathan O'Dell; cover and interior book design by Diane Kistner; Minion Pro text and ITC Avant Garde Gothic titling

About FutureCycle Press

FutureCycle Press is dedicated to publishing lasting English-language poetry books, chapbooks, and anthologies in both print-on-demand and ebook formats. Founded in 2007 by long-time independent editor/publishers and partners Diane Kistner and Robert S. King, the press incorporated as a nonprofit in 2012. A number of our editors are distinguished poets and writers in their own right, and we have been actively involved in the small press movement going back to the early seventies.

The FutureCycle Poetry Book Prize and honorarium is awarded annually for the best full-length volume of poetry we publish in a calendar year. Introduced in 2013, our Good Works projects are anthologies devoted to issues of universal significance, with all proceeds donated to a related worthy cause. Our Selected Poems series highlights contemporary poets with a substantial body of work to their credit; with this series we strive to resurrect work that has had limited distribution and is now out of print.

We are dedicated to giving all of the authors we publish the care their work deserves, making our catalog of titles the most diverse and distinguished it can be, and paying forward any earnings to fund more great books.

We've learned a few things about independent publishing over the years. We've also evolved a unique, resilient publishing model that allows us to focus mainly on vetting and preserving for posterity the most books of exceptional quality without becoming overwhelmed with bookkeeping and mailing, fundraising activities, or taxing editorial and production "bubbles." To find out more about what we are doing, come see us at www.futurecycle.org.

The FutureCycle Poetry Book Prize

All full-length volumes of poetry published by FutureCycle Press in a given calendar year are considered for the annual FutureCycle Poetry Book Prize. This allows us to consider each submission on its own merits, outside of the context of a contest. Too, the judges see the finished book, which will have benefitted from the beautiful book design and strong editorial gloss we are famous for.

The book ranked the best in judging is announced as the prize-winner in the subsequent year. There is no fixed monetary award; instead, the winning poet receives an honorarium of 20% of the total net royalties from all poetry books and chapbooks the press sold online in the year the winning book was published. The winner is also accorded the honor of being on the panel of judges for the next year's competition; all judges receive copies of all contending books to keep for their personal library.

Made in the USA
Charleston, SC
22 September 2015